# Little People, BIG DREAMS™
# ANDY WARHOL

Written by
Maria Isabel Sánchez Vegara

Illustrated by
Timothy Hunt

Frances Lincoln
Children's Books

Little Andy was the tiniest and palest child of the Warholas,
a humble couple from Slovakia who lived in Pittsburgh.
He spent every minute of his day drawing, but he was too shy
to share his work with others…even his family!

Every Sunday morning, his mother would take him to church.
Then back home, he played baseball with his brothers.
Andy always carried his sketchbook with him, and not five
minutes could pass before he was drawing again.

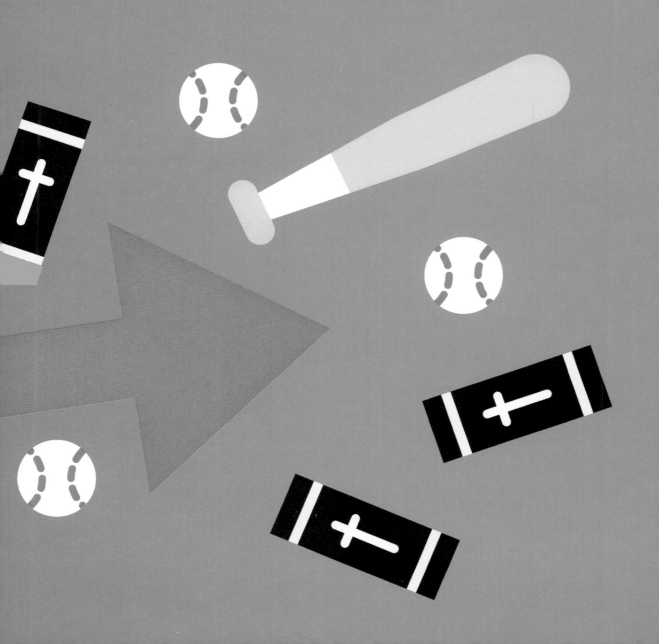

Aged eight, his legs started shaking like a marionette, and Andy had to lay in bed for months. He had a great time looking through the pages of magazines, cutting up pictures of Hollywood stars.

Trying to smile back at the faces in his collages, Andy wished he could be as charming, rich, and famous as they were.

He thought his shyness would make it hard,
but he was determined to make up for it with talent.

At the Art Club he attended, Andy felt
like an invisible man.

nchez

T. Hunt

A. Warhola

liams

K. Cotton

K. Flint

Still, when it was time to work, he made himself noticed.
By the time the rest of the students had finished
just one picture, he had put together a whole pile!

Andy won a prize at a college exhibition, for a drawing he made while helping his brother deliver groceries. It was the first time a newspaper had written an article about him. It felt good, and Andy wanted more.

WAR

He took a train to New York, where he got a chance
to publish his first illustration for a glamorous magazine.
But they accidentally dropped the 'a' of his last name.
And that's how Andy Warhola became…Andy Warhol!

HOL

Andy became known for drawing charming shoes, colorful make-up, and glamorous sunglasses for the best magazines in town. But as an artist, he liked to look at ordinary things. Especially the tomato soup he had for lunch every day.

Instead of creating just one painting—like most artists did—Andy decided to make 32 pictures of 32 soup cans. Each of them was a different flavor, but they all looked so much alike. It was hard to tell them apart!

His first exhibition looked more like a grocery store than an art gallery. Viewers were shocked by all the canvases placed in a line like products on shelves. They wondered if something so surprisingly every day could be called 'art.'

Of course it could! It was 'Pop Art'—the art for all—and soon, Andy was its king. Bottles, bills, famous faces…he produced hundreds of copies of the same pictures, and made each one unique with his interesting perspective and bright colors.

He opened a space called 'The Factory,' where the coolest musicians, actors, and models loved to hang out. But, for Andy, the hip crowd were his assistants. After all, he liked to work even when he was not working.

And by letting his art speak for him, Andy—the quiet little genius—made himself heard all around the globe.
And he showed us that even an ordinary can of tomato soup can make the whole world go 'pop!'

# ANDY WARHOL

(Born 1928 • Died 1987)

1964

1965

Born in Pittsburgh, Pennsylvania, in August 1928, Andrew Warhola was
the youngest of three brothers. His parents, Andrew and Julia, emigrated
to the USA from the Slovak Republic in the 1920s. The Warhol siblings
grew up in a smoky, industrial city during the Great Depression, where
Andy learnt to draw. Aged six, he was confined to bed with sickness. With
nothing else to do, he turned to images from magazines and newspapers,
tracing them and cutting them out. At high school, Andy furthered his
interest in art and design, and was the first member of his family to go to
college. One summer, he worked dressing window displays, where he fell
in love with high fashion. This also sparked an interest in illustration, which
he went on to study at the Carnegie Institute. The night of graduation,

1971                                    1980

he caught a train to New York…and never left. Picking up illustration
work for magazines such as Vogue, Andy caught the eye of art directors
everywhere. Aged 32, he bought a four-storey townhouse and started
to experiment with fine art, using newspaper images and advertising to
make his own art. Turning soup cans into large scale screenprints, he also
reimagined portraits of icons such as Marilyn Monroe, Jackie Kennedy,
and Elvis. In doing so he became one of the world's most influential 'pop'
artists, celebrating the idea that anything can be art. Andy went on to
set up a studio called 'The Factory,' which became a hub for artists. He
became world-famous, exhibiting both screenprints and film. Today, he
is remembered as the artist who found beauty in everyday objects.

Want to find out more about **Andy Warhol?**

Have a read of these great books:

*Uncle Andy's* by James Warhola

*Who Was Andy Warhol?* by Kirsten Anderson

Brimming with creative inspiration, how-to projects, and useful information to enrich your everyday life, Quarto Knows is a favourite destination for those pursuing their interests and passions. Visit our site and dig deeper with our books into your area of interest: Quarto Creates, Quarto Cooks, Quarto Homes, Quarto Lives, Quarto Drives, Quarto Explores, Quarto Gifts, or Quarto Kids.

Text © 2021 Maria Isabel Sánchez Vegara. Illustrations © 2021 Timothy Hunt

Original concept of the series by Maria Isabel Sánchez Vegara, published by Alba Editorial, s.l.u

Produced under trademark licence from Alba Editorial s.l.u and Beautifool Couple S.L.

First Published in the US in 2021 by Frances Lincoln Children's Books, an imprint of The Quarto Group.

100 Cummings Center, Suite 265D, Beverly, MA 01915, USA.

T +1 978-282-9590 **www.QuartoKnows.com**

ISBN 978-0-7112-5795-5

Set in Futura BT.

Published by Katie Cotton • Designed by Karissa Santos

Edited by Katy Flint • Editorial Assistance from Alex Hithersay

Production by Nikki Ingram

Manufactured in Guangdong, China CC022021

1 3 5 7 9 8 6 4 2

Photographic acknowledgements (pages 28-29, from left to right) 1. Portrait of the American artist Andy Warhol. New York, 1964 © Mario De Biasi/Mondadori via Getty Images 2. American pop artist Andy Warhol (1928 – 1987) with a vintage plate camera on a tripod, ca. 1965 © Popperfoto via Getty Images 3. Andy Warhol at his May 1971 retrospective at the Whitney Museum of American Art, New York © Jack Mitchell/Getty Images 4. Andy Warhol, 1980 © A. Unangst Ltd/Corbis via Getty Images.

# Collect the Little People, BIG DREAMS™ series:

| | | | | | |
|---|---|---|---|---|---|
| **FRIDA KAHLO**  | **COCO CHANEL**  | **MAYA ANGELOU**  | **AMELIA EARHART**  | **AGATHA CHRISTIE**  | **MARIE CURIE**  |
| **ROSA PARKS**  | **AUDREY HEPBURN**  | **EMMELINE PANKHURST**  | **ELLA FITZGERALD**  | **ADA LOVELACE**  | **JANE AUSTEN**  |
| **GEORGIA O'KEEFFE**  | **HARRIET TUBMAN**  | **ANNE FRANK**  | **MOTHER TERESA**  | **JOSEPHINE BAKER**  | **L. M. MONTGOMERY**  |
| **JANE GOODALL**  | **SIMONE DE BEAUVOIR**  | **MUHAMMAD ALI**  | **STEPHEN HAWKING**  | **MARIA MONTESSORI**  | **VIVIENNE WESTWOOD**  |
| **MAHATMA GANDHI**  | **DAVID BOWIE**  | **WILMA RUDOLPH**  | **DOLLY PARTON**  | **BRUCE LEE**  | **RUDOLF NUREYEV**  |
| **ZAHA HADID**  | **MARY SHELLEY**  | **MARTIN LUTHER KING JR.**  | **DAVID ATTENBOROUGH**  | **ASTRID LINDGREN**  | **EVONNE GOOLAGONG**  |

**BOB DYLAN**

**ALAN TURING**

**BILLIE JEAN KING**

**GRETA THUNBERG**

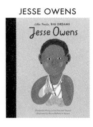

**JESSE OWENS**

**JEAN-MICHEL BASQUIAT**

**ARETHA FRANKLIN**

**CORAZON AQUINO**

**PELÉ**

**ERNEST SHACKLETON**

**STEVE JOBS**

**AYRTON SENNA**

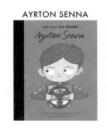

**LOUISE BOURGEOIS**

**ELTON JOHN**

**JOHN LENNON**

**PRINCE**

**CHARLES DARWIN**

**CAPTAIN TOM MOORE**

**HANS CHRISTIAN ANDERSEN**

**STEVIE WONDER**

**MEGAN RAPINOE**

**MARY ANNING**

**MALALA YOUSAFZAI**

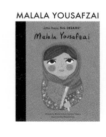

**ANDY WARHOL**

**RUPAUL**

# ACTIVITY BOOKS

**STICKER ACTIVITY BOOK**

**COLORING BOOK**

**LITTLE ME, BIG DREAMS JOURNAL**

Discover more about the series at www.littlepeoplebigdreams.com